FEB 26 2003

Picture the Past
Life in
St. Augustine

Sally Senzell Isaacs

Heinemann Library
Chicago, Illinois

Produced for Heinemann Library by
    Bender Richardson White.
Editor: Lionel Bender
Designer and Media Conversion: Ben White
Picture Researcher: Cathy Stastny
Production Controller: Kim Richardson

07 06 05 04 03
10 9 8 7 6 5 4 3 2 1

Printed and bound in the United States by
    Lake Book Manufacturing, Inc.

Library of Congress Cataloging-in-Publication Data.
Isaacs, Sally Senzell, 1950-
    Life in St. Augustine / Sally Senzell Isaacs.
        p. cm. -- (Picture the past)
Includes index.
Summary: An overview of life in St. Augustine, Florida,
from 1513 to 1845, including the housing, food, clothing,
schools, and everyday activities of the settlers, as well as
their interaction with native people.
    ISBN 1-58810-694-2 (HC), 1-40340-526-3 (Pbk)
    1. Saint Augustine (Fla.)--History--Juvenile literature.
2. Saint Augustine (Fla.)--Social life and customs--
Juvenile literature. 3. Spaniards--Florida--Saint Augustine--
History--Juvenile literature. 4. Timucua Indians--Florida--
Saint Augustine--History--Juvenile literature. (1. Saint
Augustine (Fla.)--History. 2. Saint Augustine (Fla.)--Social
life and customs. 3. Spaniards--Florida--History. 4.
Timucua Indians. 5. Indians of North America--Florida. 6.
Castillo de San Marcos (Saint Augustine, Fla.) 7. Florida--
History--To 1821. 8. Florida--History--1821-1865.) I. Title.
    F319.S2 I83 2002
    975.9'18--dc21
                                2002000793

Special thanks to Angela McHaney Brown at Heinemann
Library for editorial and design guidance and direction.

Acknowledgments
The producers and publishers are grateful to the
following for permission to reproduce copyright material:
Tristan Boyer Binns: pages 3, 15, 19, 23, 24, 30. Corbis
Images: Dave G. Houser, pages 1, 20, 22; James L. Amos,
page 11; Bettmann Archive, pages 10, 17, 28; Richard
Cummins, page 21; Nik Wheeler, page 14; Corbis, page
6. Peter Newark's American Pictures: pages 7, 8, 16, 29.
North Wind Pictures: pages 12, 13, 27.
Cover photograph: James L. Amos/Corbis Images.

Illustrations on pages 4, 9, 18, 25, and 26 by John James.
Map by Stefan Chabluk.

ABOUT THIS BOOK

This book tells about life in
St. Augustine, Florida, from 1513
to 1845. St. Augustine is often
called the oldest city in the United
States. It is actually the oldest
permanent city in the continental
United States settled by people
from Europe. It is important to
remember that **Native Americans**
lived in villages across the country
long before the Spanish explorers
arrived in
St. Augustine.

We have illustrated the book
with artists' ideas of how things
looked in early St. Augustine.
We also include modern
photographs of places that remain
from the early days.

The Author

Sally Senzell Isaacs is a professional writer
and editor of nonfiction books for children.
She graduated from Indiana University,
earning a B.S. degree in Education with
majors in American History and Sociology.
Sally Senzell Isaacs has written more than
30 history books for children.

Note to the Reader

Some words are shown in bold, **like
this.** You can find out what they mean
by looking in the glossary.

CONTENTS

The New World

Christopher Columbus landed on islands near Florida in 1492. He returned to Spain with news about a "new world." Columbus was sure there was gold and spices in the new world, which he still thought was in the Indies, near Japan. Soon more explorers set out from Spain. Juan Ponce de León was one of the first to reach the southeastern part of North America. He landed on April 2, 1513, a day called the "feast of flowers" in Spain. He named the land after *florida,* the Spanish word for "flowery."

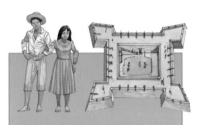

Look for these
The illustration of a Spanish boy and girl shows you the subject of each double-page story in the book.
The illustration of the Castillo de San Marcos marks boxes with interesting facts about life in St. Augustine.

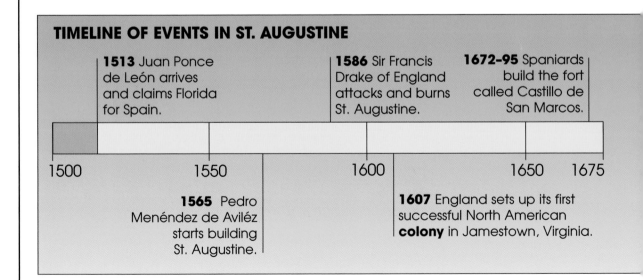

TIMELINE OF EVENTS IN ST. AUGUSTINE

1513 Juan Ponce de León arrives and claims Florida for Spain.

1586 Sir Francis Drake of England attacks and burns St. Augustine.

1672–95 Spaniards build the fort called Castillo de San Marcos.

| 1500 | 1550 | 1600 | 1650 | 1675 |

1565 Pedro Menéndez de Aviléz starts building St. Augustine.

1607 England sets up its first successful North American **colony** in Jamestown, Virginia.

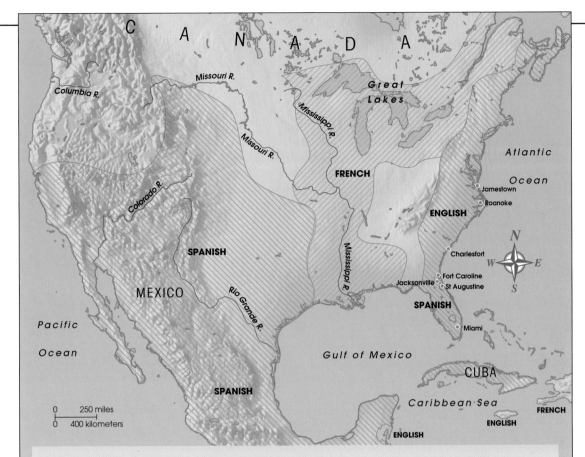

By 1700, Spain, France, and England had **claimed** land in North America. When an explorer found land, he claimed it by saying it belonged to his country. Some claims overlapped.

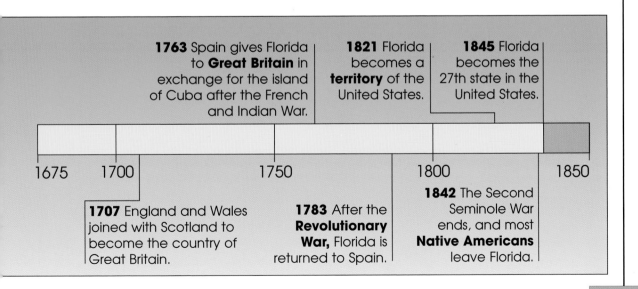

1763 Spain gives Florida to **Great Britain** in exchange for the island of Cuba after the French and Indian War.

1821 Florida becomes a **territory** of the United States.

1845 Florida becomes the 27th state in the United States.

1675   1700   1750   1800   1850

1707 England and Wales joined with Scotland to become the country of Great Britain.

1783 After the **Revolutionary War,** Florida is returned to Spain.

1842 The Second Seminole War ends, and most **Native Americans** leave Florida.

The First People

When the Spanish people arrived in Florida, there were between 10,000 and 25,000 **Native Americans** living there. They lived in many different groups, called nations. The nation that lived near St. Augustine was called Timucua.

The Timucuan women made pottery, grew corn, and prepared food. The men fished, hunted alligators and deer for food, and fought with enemy nations.

Florida's Native Americans built their homes with the trunks of pine trees and the leaves of palm trees.

When the Spanish ships landed, the Timucuas were friendly. They shared their food and their homes. A Timucuan leader even allowed a Spanish explorer to use the Council House, a very important building.

But by 1565, the Spanish people wanted to take over the land. They forced the Timucuas to build the town of St. Augustine, search for gold, and plant food. Many Timucuas later died from diseases that were brought over from Europe or Africa.

The Timucuas made their clothing from animal skins. Men wore very little clothing. They pierced their ears and wore earrings. Here they are spearing fish in a stream.

7

St. Augustine Begins

Both France and Spain wanted a **colony** in Florida. A colony is like a small, new town. It is built in one country by people from a different country. French and African soldiers arrived first and built Fort Caroline in 1564. Spain's King Philip the Second was angry to hear this news. He sent out Pedro Menéndez de Aviléz with 600 soldiers and 100 **settlers.** Their job was to destroy the French **Protestant** colony and start a Spanish **Roman Catholic** colony.

A French artist, Jacques Le Moyne, visited the French colony of Fort Caroline and drew this picture. Spanish soldiers destroyed the colony a year and a half after it was built.

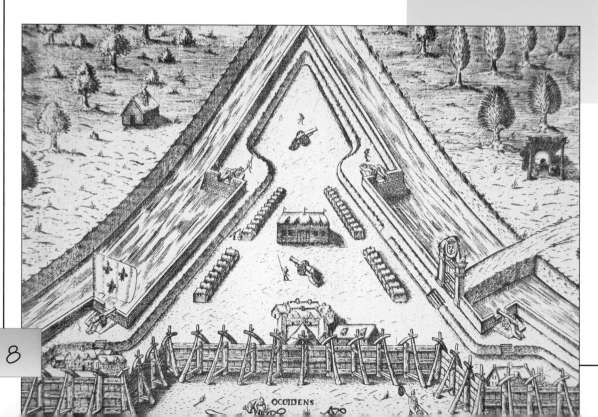

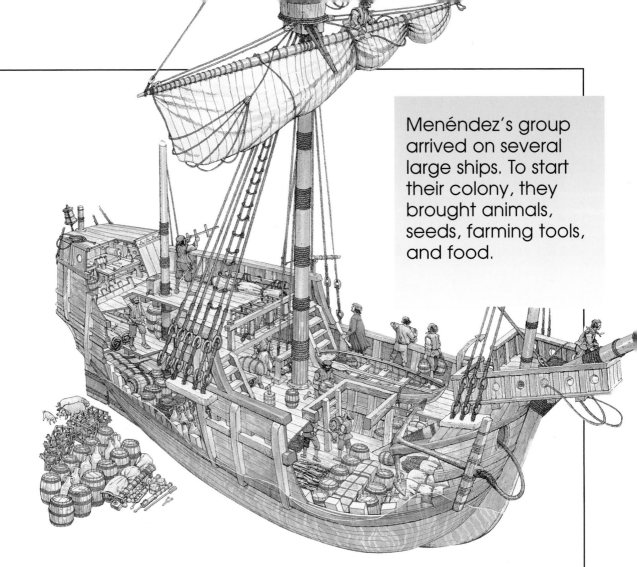

Menéndez's group arrived on several large ships. To start their colony, they brought animals, seeds, farming tools, and food.

On September 6, 1565, Menéndez and his soldiers landed in Florida. Menéndez announced that the land belonged to Spain. Because he had spotted land on August 28, the feast day of Saint Augustine, he named the colony St. Augustine. Then he led his soldiers to Fort Caroline over land through a storm. When they arrived, they burned the buildings and killed most of the French soldiers.

WHO WAS SAINT AUGUSTINE?

He lived in the years 354 to 430. He was a Christian **religious** leader and teacher in what is now the North African country of Algeria.

Hard Times

The first years the Spaniards spent in St. Augustine were filled with struggles with the **Native Americans** and pirate attacks. There were also mosquitoes, hunger, and storms. The Spanish soldiers hunted for food, but there was not always enough. Hurricanes blew through St. Augustine, destroying their huts. Many Spaniards died in these first years. Others asked to be allowed to go back to Spain.

This is a map of St. Augustine from 1588. It shows Sir Francis Drake's 1586 attack on St. Augustine.

The Spanish soldiers needed to protect Spain's land in Florida. Having control of the land meant that they could protect Spanish ships carrying silver and gold from Mexico and Peru. Both France and England wanted to **claim** Florida. In 1586, Sir Francis Drake of England led the first of many attacks on St. Augustine. In 1695, the Spanish finished building a strong fort called Castillo (kas-TEE-yoh) de San Marcos, which means Castle of Saint Mark.

This is Castillo de San Marcos. When the English attacked in 1702, about 1,500 townspeople ran inside for protection. They stayed there safely for 58 days while the English robbed and burned the rest of St. Augustine.

11

Building a Town

By 1695, the Castillo was complete. Later, the townspeople built walls around the town to keep out enemies. After many years, houses, shops, churches, and offices were built around a **plaza.** In the center of the plaza was a market where people bought food and other goods. They also had parties in the plaza.

The Spanish soldiers carefully planned how to lay out the streets of St. Augustine. They used ropes as guidelines to help make a map of the town.

Priests of the **Roman Catholic religion** came to St. Augustine to set up **missions.** They named one mission *Nombre de Dios*, which means "Name of God." It was the first mission in the United States. The priests encouraged people of the Timucua nation to come to the mission and **convert** to the Catholic religion.

To get from one part of town to another, people walked. They used mules to carry things. To travel farther, people paddled canoes on the rivers.

MISSION DAYS

The Timucuas usually lived in villages around the mission. They came to the mission for prayer services, classes, and to work. Mission days ended by 1763. By then, there were very few **Native Americans** left in St. Augustine.

Homes

Houses did not have front doors. People walked through a gate to a patio. They entered the house through a back or side door.

After storms and fires destroyed the first wooden houses, people built stronger homes with *coquina*. This is a rocky material made of tiny seashells. Neither wind nor fire could destroy coquina.

This is the Gonzalez-Alvarez house. It is now open to visitors. It was built in the early 1700s and was home to many different families through the 1800s and early 1900s.

Many homes had only two rooms plus an outdoor porch. There were no closets. People hung their clothes on nails. They had a chest to store things and to sit on, a simple dining table, and mats that were unrolled at night for sleeping. For light at night, people burned olive or fish oil in lamps.

KITCHENS

Most houses had outdoor kitchens. This kept the house cooler. Also, if there was a fire in the kitchen, it did not harm the rest of the house.

Adults at Work

By the early 1700s, St. Augustine was a busy town. Because it was near the sea, ships coming from Mexico and Cuba stopped there to deliver goods. It was also the place where soldiers from enemy ships tried to attack Florida. Many St. Augustine men were soldiers. Spaniards, African **slaves,** and **Native Americans** watched for enemies coming by sea or land.

People came to meet the arriving ships. Many of the workers were African slaves or Native Americans. These workers often were paid in corn flour or meat.

When soldiers were not on duty, they had other jobs. Many were **blacksmiths,** builders, farmers, or fishermen. Women prepared meals, sewed clothing, and cared for the children. To earn extra money, some women cooked and cleaned in the homes of wealthy people.

This blacksmith is at work in his workshop. As well as making and fitting horseshoes, the blacksmith made metal tools, nails, and lamps.

A Child's Day

Children had many jobs at home. They took care of animals and gathered eggs from the chickens. They often helped their mothers prepare food. Every day they crushed kernels of corn to make flour for baking.

These children are working and playing outside their house. The bars on the windows are called *rejas*. They allow fresh air in, but keep strangers out. They were most often on the street side of the house.

By age ten, boys learned a craft by working with a skilled builder or **blacksmith**. At age fifteen, most boys became soldiers. Girls helped their mothers cook and sew. Many girls got married at age thirteen.

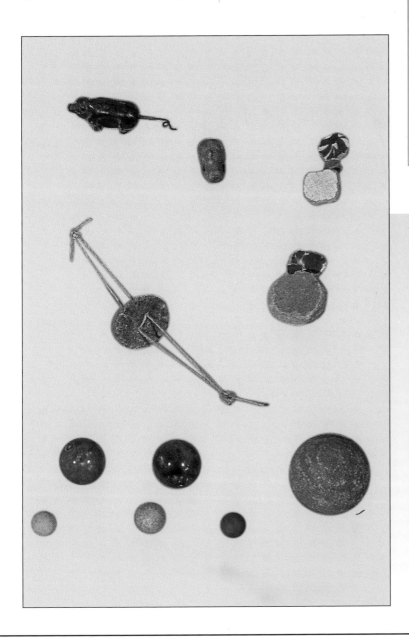

NAP TIME

Children and adults ate their biggest meal at noon. Then they rested until the temperature cooled off. The rest time is called a *siesta*. After the siesta, people returned to work.

Archaeologists have found pieces of children's toys buried in the ground at St. Augustine. They tell us that children played with marbles, animals carved from metal or stone, and wizzers, which make noise.

School

Since the early 1600s, children in St. Augustine went to school. **Priests** were the teachers. They taught lessons in **religion,** reading, writing, and arithmetic. **Native Americans** went to school at the **mission.** Wealthy families paid priests to teach their children privately at home.

This one-room school in St. Augustine is one of the oldest wooden schoolhouses in the United States. The teacher lived upstairs.

THE OLDEST WOODEN
SCHOOL HOUSE IN THE U.S.

This is a display of a teacher and students in the wooden schoolhouse in St. Augustine. Older children sat on wooden benches. Younger children sat on little stools.

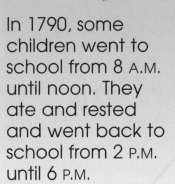

SCHOOL DAY

In 1790, some children went to school from 8 A.M. until noon. They ate and rested and went back to school from 2 P.M. until 6 P.M.

In 1790, Florida was ruled by the King of Spain. Spain's King Carlos the Fourth ordered that all boys go to school for free. This was the first school in the United States to allow African-American boys to be in the same classes as white boys. Girls began going to school in the 1800s.

21

Clothes

In the 1600s and 1700s, most women sewed clothes by hand for their families. Men, women, and children slept in long shirts. In the morning, they put their dresses or pants over the shirts. Zippers had not been invented. Clothing had laces or buttons.

These women are wearing the colorful, long dresses worn by Spanish women in St. Augustine in the 1700s.

Soldiers wore uniforms like these at Castillo de San Marcos.

BUTTONS AND POCKETS

● To pass the time, soldiers carved buttons out of cow bones.

● In the 1600s, a woman wore a pocket attached to a band around her waist. Pockets were not sewn into skirts until the 1700s.

Women wore long dresses with vests and aprons. A scarf protected their hair. Men wore knee-length pants. Children dressed like their parents. Clothing cost a lot of money. Each person had only one or two changes of clothing.

23

Food and Cooking

Each family had a small garden by its house. People grew beans, corn, squash, peppers, tomatoes, and pumpkins. Fig, peach, and orange trees grew in the yard. Many people raised cows, goats, and chickens for food. To buy food, such as flour, coffee, or fish, people shopped at markets in the **plaza.**

This is a stove from the 1740s. Wood was burned inside the two front holes. A pot of food was cooked on top. After the wood burned, someone swept out the stove and baked bread in the hot, empty hole.

St. Augustine Recipe—Hot Chocolate

Hot chocolate was a popular breakfast drink in Spain, Mexico, and Florida. Explorers from Spain learned about the cocoa trees from the **Native Americans** in Mexico. You can make a similar drink with this recipe.

WARNING: Do not cook anything unless there is an adult to help you. Always ask an adult to help you cook at the stove and to handle hot liquids.

YOU WILL NEED
1/4 cup unsweetened cocoa
1/2 cup sugar
1 tablespoon flour
1/2 teaspoon salt
1 teaspoon cinnamon
1 cup cold water
4 cups milk
1 teaspoon vanilla extract

FOLLOW THE STEPS

1. Pour the cocoa, sugar, flour, salt, cinnamon, and water into a pan.
2. Cook the mixture over low heat. Stir until the dry ingredients dissolve into the water.

3. Turn the heat to medium high and stir until the mixture boils. Turn down the heat a little and boil for about four minutes, stirring all the time.

4. Add the milk and continue to stir until the milk is very hot, but not boiling.
5. Remove the pan from the heat and stir in the vanilla extract.
   Serves 4 to 6 people.

25

Britain Takes Over

Around 1760, Britain, Spain, and France were fighting over land in North America and the Caribbean. The war was called the French and Indian War. **Native Americans** helped soldiers on both sides. Spain supported the French soldiers. In the war, Britain took Cuba, a Spanish island near Florida. When Britain won the war in 1763, Spain gave Florida to Britain so Cuba could be returned to Spain.

Native Americans and French soldiers are attacking these British soldiers in their bright red coats. By the end of the war, the British had taken control of all French colonies in North America.

26

When Britain took over Florida, many of the people living in St. Augustine moved to Cuba. British **settlers** moved in.

The British stayed only twenty years. By 1783, they had lost the **Revolutionary War** against their North American **colonies.** Britain had to return Florida to Spain. After the war, only 50 Spanish people moved back to St. Augustine.

At different times, Spain, Britain, and the United States have **claimed** St. Augustine. The flags of these countries still fly alongside the state flag of Florida.

Americans Move In

By 1803, all the land around Florida belonged to the United States. Spain knew that soon the United States would want Florida, too. In 1821, Spain let the United States buy Florida. That year Florida became a U.S. **territory.** In 1845, Florida became a state.

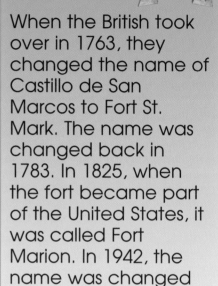

NAMING THE FORT

When the British took over in 1763, they changed the name of Castillo de San Marcos to Fort St. Mark. The name was changed back in 1783. In 1825, when the fort became part of the United States, it was called Fort Marion. In 1942, the name was changed back again to Castillo de San Marcos.

Every year, Americans took over more **Native American** land. The U.S. Army had a variety of uniforms and was equipped with horses and rifles.

By the 1830s, thousands of Native Americans in the eastern states left their land. Many were weak from battles and disease. Others were forced out by the U.S. Army. Many of them went to Oklahoma, an "Indian **Territory,"** which was land set aside for them by the U.S. **government.**

But the Seminoles of Florida would not leave. From 1817 to 1858, they fought the U.S. Army. Finally, most Seminoles left for Oklahoma.

NUMBERS

In 1835, there had been 5,000 Seminoles in Florida. By 1842, about 400 had been killed and 4,000 had agreed to move to Indian Territory. The 600 that were left hid in the swamps.

This is Osceola, one of the leaders of the Seminoles. In 1837, an army officer asked to meet him. When Osceola showed up, soldiers tricked him and put him in prison at Castillo de San Marcos in St. Augustine. Soon they moved him to a prison in South Carolina. He died there in 1838.

St. Augustine Today

The people of St. Augustine are proud of their past. They have rebuilt houses, stores, and buildings to look as they did centuries ago. The site of the **mission,** the Castillo, and historic houses are open to the public. Visitors can step back into the long history of this very old city.

Visitors can walk across this bridge at the Castillo de San Marcos. In the early days, soldiers walked across the bridge, and then raised it so enemies could not cross it.

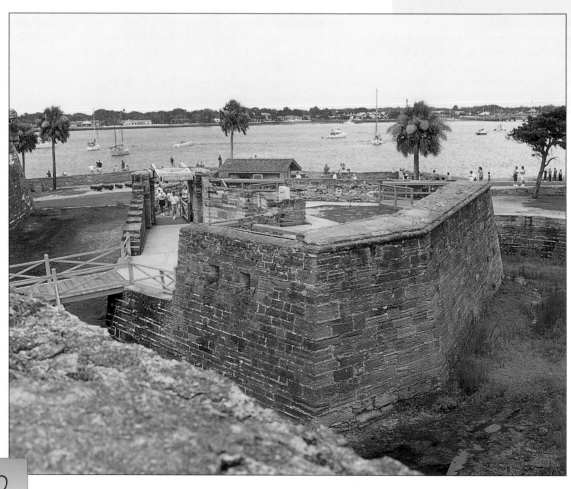

Glossary

archaeologist person who learns about the past by digging up old objects

blacksmith person who makes tools and other things from iron

claim to say that something belongs to you or your country

colony small, new town that is built in one country by people from a different country

convert to change from one religion to another

government people who make rules for a country

Great Britain country formed in 1707 by England, Scotland, and Wales. The country is also called Britain and the people are called British.

mission place where people live, work, study, and pray together

Native Americans groups, or nations, of people who lived in North and South America before 1492

plaza open area in the center of a town

priest in certain religions, someone who can lead services and perform ceremonies

Protestant belonging to the Christian religion that broke away from the Catholic church

religion system of belief in a god or gods

Revolutionary War (1775–1783) war in which the North American colonies won independence from Great Britain

Roman Catholic belonging to the religion whose leader is the pope

settler person who makes a new home in a new place

slave person who was owned by another person and made to work without pay

territory part of the United States that has not yet become a state

---

More Books to Read

Cooper, Jason. *Historic St. Augustine.* Vero Beach, Fla.: Rourke Book Company, 2000.

Yacowitz, Carolyn Huberman. *The Seminole.* Chicago: Heinemann Library, 2002.

An older reader can help you read this book:

Binns, Tristan Boyer. *St. Augustine.* Chicago: Heinemann Library, 2001.

Index